For too long, beauty has been defined by narrow, unattainable stereotypes. It's time to change all that. Because Dove believes real beauty comes in many shapes, sizes, colors and ages. It's why we started the campaign for real beauty. And why we hope you'll take part. Together, let's think, talk, debate and learn how to make beauty real again. Cast your vote at campaignforrealbeauty.com

"Our beliefs can move us forward in life—or they can hold us back."

ou become what
you believe—not what you wish or want but what you truly
believe. Wherever you are in life, look at your beliefs.
They put you there.

When I was growing up in Mississippi in the 1950s, I
never believed what people said about being poor or
black or female. I would overhear my family talking about
the dire circumstances for blacks, but I never believed
that would be my life.

I believed I belonged to someone or something bigger
than myself, my family, or even Mississippi. I believed
I was God's child. Therefore, I could do anything.

I can still remember a cold winter day when I was
4 years old. I was helping to churn butter on the back
porch and watching my grandmother lift clothes from

"But you—you don't understand," I sobbed. To this day, I can't remember what it was that had me so far gone, which only proves the point Maya was trying to make. "I do understand," she told me. "I want to hear you say it now. Out loud. 'Thank you.'" Tentatively, I repeated it: "Thank you—but what am I saying thank you for?"

"You're saying thank you," Maya said, "because your faith is so strong that you don't doubt that whatever the problem, you'll get through it. You're saying thank you because you know that even in the eye of the storm, God has put a rainbow in the clouds. You're saying thank you because you know there's no problem created that can compare to the Creator of all things. Say thank you!"

So I did—and still do. Only now I do it every day. I keep a gratitude journal, as Sarah Ban Breathnach suggests in *Simple Abundance,* listing at least five things that I'm grateful for. My list includes small pleasures: the feel of Kentucky bluegrass under my feet (like damp silk); a walk in the woods with all nine of my dogs and my cocker spaniel Sophie trying to keep up; cooking fried green tomatoes with Stedman and eating them while they're hot; reading a good book and knowing another awaits.

My thank-you list also includes things too important to take for granted: an "okay" mammogram, friends who love me, 15 years at the same job (and loving it more than the first day I started), a chance to share my vision for a better life, staying centered, having financial security. I won't kid you, having money for all the things I want is a blessing. But as I look back over my journals, which

I've kept since I was 15 years old, 99 percent of what brought me real joy had nothing to do with money. (It had *a lot* to do with food, however.)

It's not easy being grateful all the time. But it's when you feel least thankful that you are most in need of what gratitude can give you: perspective. Just knowing you have that daily list to complete allows you to look at your day differently, with an awareness of every sweet gesture and kind thought passed your way. When you learn to say thank you, you see the world anew. And as Meister Eckhart so eloquently stated: "If the only prayer you ever say in your whole life is 'Thank you,' that would suffice."

Most of us are certainly uncomfortable with, if not terrified of, failure. We think it defines us. It does not. Like every other experience, failure is defined by our reaction to it. Failures can be God's little whispers; other times, they are full earthquakes erupting in our lives because we didn't listen to the whispers. Failure is just a way for our lives to show us that we're moving in the wrong direction, that we should try something different. It holds no more power than we give it.

I learned this lesson all too well after the release of the movie *Beloved,* my beloved project that took me ten years to make and that I still count as one of the greatest accomplishments of my life. It made $23 million at the box office—by Hollywood standards, a failure. I was disheartened and depressed. It took me months to recover and come to my senses, to realize that Hollywood's standards are not my own.

I had the most beautiful team in the world: director Jonathan Demme, who will be a friend forever, and a cast and crew to rejoice over. We had the guts to follow our vision and make the movie we thought the world deserved to see. To this day, I wouldn't take back a day in the making of it. I was sooo happy, so fulfilled.

So what is the problem? I kept asking myself after we were beaten by *Bride of Chucky* the first weekend. The problem was not the movie we made but my attachment to the outcome.

"What was your intention?" my friend Gary Zukav asked me one night when I called to lament the poor turnout. My intention was to create a movie so powerful that it would allow people to feel, not just see, what it meant to overcome slavery and be able to love—and to reconstruct a life. My intention was for people to realize that this wasn't just a "period" in history, that these were real people, my ancestors, who had fought their way back to some sense of humanity in ordinary and extraordinary ways. "Well," Gary said, "you did that."

That was when I realized that I hadn't taken into account all the people who didn't want to feel what I felt. In that moment, I was willing to give up my expectation for box office numbers and just look at the work. I let go of my sadness. I started to feel grateful for every person who saw the movie and felt moved and got in touch with their own humanity.

The lessons I learned from making the film and the depth of feelings I have for my history, for the strength and courage of those who came before me, expanded me in ways I still can't fully express. The experience opened me up to know that if my ancestors could survive with so little, then I, who have been given so much, can surely be triumphant. No box office returns can ever diminish that.

But the greatest lesson from that experience is to do your best, enjoy the journey, and then release all attachment to what is to come. Let it be. And be comfortable with whatever it is.

to change my mind." She said, "Who else would? It's *your* mind."

Before then, I hadn't thought of changing my mind as even possible. What about honor, commitment, staying the course? I had always believed that going back on a promise was something only careless, flaky people did. Yet as strict as I had always been about keeping my word, I often gave it irresponsibly. Trying to be the nice girl, I agreed to do things I later regretted. And because I was saying yes when I really meant no, I'd end up cheating both myself and the other person involved. It's an irrefutable law of the universe: You always get exactly what you intend—and my intention was to be seen by others as the dependable one, even if that came at a high expense to me personally.

What I know for sure is that you have the right to choose what is best for yourself *now*—not four years ago or even yesterday. And changing your mind does not mean acting irresponsibly; it's just the opposite. When you honor what you know your spirit is telling you to do, you are making the most conscientious decision, one for which you are willing to accept all the consequences. You understand that when you know better, you ought to do better—and doing better sometimes means changing your mind; and you realize that letting go of what others think you should do is the only way to reach your full potential.

A business student of mine once challenged me on this concept. "I'm passionate about cooking," she explained, "but my parents have spent nearly $100,000 on my education. For me to now announce that I want to cook…. How can I change my mind?" I said, "Is $100,000 worth a life not fulfilled? How much of your life will you have to consume before you can please *you*?"

Every day, passion speaks to us through our feelings. That's why when you allow yourself to become anesthetized by what others think, you literally block yourself from living the life you were called to live. I promise you that if you make a choice that doesn't please your mate, your friends, your mother, or *whoever*, the world will not fall apart—the people who truly love you want you to love yourself. And as you become clearer about who you really are, you'll be better able to decide what is best for you—the first time around.

"Your life is a journey of learning to love yourself first and then extending that love to others in every encounter."

JULY 2001

Think back for a moment on your history—not just where you were born but the circumstances that contributed to your being here. Consider what you believed about yourself based on what others told you directly and indirectly, since 93 percent of communication is through nuance and action, not words. How were you treated? That is what defined how you experienced the world—both the moments when you felt valued and wanted and the moments when you felt wounded and sure you'd never be fulfilled. Though you've probably had times when you didn't want to press on, you have survived your path. You are still here, still standing— and what an amazing journey your life has been!

No matter who we are or where we live, we all have our own journey. Mine began the moment I was conceived out of wedlock to Vernon Winfrey and Vernita Lee, who happened by an oak tree one April afternoon in 1953 in rural Mississippi. Their onetime union, not at all a romance, brought about the unwanted pregnancy that was me. Relatives tell me that my mother concealed her pregnancy until the day I was born—so no one was prepared for my arrival. There were no baby showers, none of the anticipation of delight that I see in the faces of my expectant friends who rub their swollen stomachs with reverence. My birth was surrounded with regret, shame, and hiding.

I marvel at what it must feel like to be born into a world where people lovingly greet you and celebrate your arrival. As far back as I can recall, I felt the need to show that I belonged here—the need to prove my worth. I worked hard. I got A's. I became an orator, won speaking contests, earned scholarships. The words I heard Jesse Jackson say at an assembly when I was 16 became my mantra: "Excellence is the best deterrent to racism. Excellence is the best deterrent to sexism. Be excellent." I was in my mid-30s before I realized that just being born makes you worthy enough to be here. I had nothing to prove.

Even if you lived through a childhood more challenging than my own, there is one irrefutable law of the universe: We are each responsible for our own life—no other person is or even *can* be. Like me, you might have experienced things that caused you to judge yourself unworthy. It's important to know why and how you were programmed to feel the way you do so you can do the work of changing the program.

That is one of the most important challenges of your life—to heal the wounds of your past so you don't continue to bleed. Until you do, you are literally dragging the weight of your past into your present. And that makes it nearly impossible to move forward.

What I know for sure is that your life is a multipart series of all your experiences—and each experience is created by your thoughts, intentions, and actions to teach you what you most need to know. Your life is a journey of learning to love yourself first and then extending that love to others in every encounter. How can you travel on that road without fear? Whenever I'm faced with a difficult decision, I ask myself: *What would I do if I weren't afraid of making a mistake, feeling rejected, looking foolish, or being alone?* Remove the fear, and the answer comes into focus.

If you're holding anyone else accountable for your happiness, you're wasting time. You must be fearless enough to give yourself the love you didn't receive. Begin noticing how every day brings a new opportunity for your growth. How buried disagreements with your mother show up in arguments with your spouse. How unconscious feelings of unworthiness appear in everything you do and don't do. All these experiences are your life's way of making itself whole—sometimes whispering, often screaming. Pay attention. Every choice gives you a chance to pave your own road. Keep moving. Full speed ahead.

"In all my triumphs—
in every good and
great thing that has
ever happened to me—
Gayle has been my
boldest cheerleader."

AUGUST
2001

wenty-five years ago this summer, I met my best friend, Gayle King. I was a news anchor at a station in Baltimore, she was a production assistant—each of us from groups that rarely interacted and certainly weren't friendly. From the day we met, Gayle made it known how proud she was that I had the exalted position of anchorwoman and how excited she was to be part of a team I was on. It has been that way ever since.

We didn't become friends right away—we were just two women respectful and supportive of each other's path. Then one night after a big snowstorm, Gayle couldn't get home, so I invited her to stay at my place. Her biggest concern? Underwear. She was determined to drive 40 miles through a snowstorm to get to Chevy Chase,

Maryland, where she lived with her mom, in order to have clean panties. "I have lots of clean underwear," I told her. "You can use mine, or we can go buy you some." Once I finally convinced her to come home with me, we stayed up the whole night talking. And with the exception of a few times during vacations spent out of the country, Gayle and I have talked every day since.

We laugh a lot, mostly about ourselves. She has helped me through demotions, near firings, sexual harassment, and the twisted and messed-up relationships of my 20s, when I couldn't tell the difference between myself and a doormat. Night after night, Gayle listened to the latest woeful tale of how I'd been stood up, lied to, done wrong. She'd always ask for details (we call it "book, chapter, and verse"), then seem as engaged as if it were happening to her. She never judged me. Yet when I'd let some man use me, she'd often say, "He's just chipping away at your spirit. One day I hope he chips deep enough for you to see who you really are—someone who deserves to be happy."

In all my triumphs—in every good and great thing that has ever happened to me—Gayle has been my boldest cheerleader. In 1978, when I was promoted to talk show host after being demoted from news, no one was happier or more confident that I could do the job than Gayle. Then when I was offered the chance to go to Chicago and host a show in the same time slot as then–talk show king Phil Donahue, she said, "You should go to Chicago! You can beat Donahue—I know you can." "Beat Donahue?!?!" I exclaimed. "That's impossible! That's not even a goal."

I've become well known—and I've watched Gayle stand with me in a crowd, ushering autograph seekers my way, delighted that people want my name on a piece of paper, a matchbook, a napkin. I've made lots of money—and Gayle still worries that I'm spending too much. "Remember M.C. Hammer," she chides, again telling me of the rapper who went bankrupt. And in all our 25 years together, I have never sensed even a split second of jealousy from her. She loves her life with her family, school functions, and discount shopping—she will still drive across town for a sale on Tide. Only once has she admitted to wanting to trade places with me—the night I sang onstage with Tina Turner. She, who cannot carry a tune in a church pew, fantasizes about being a singer.

Gayle is the nicest person I know—genuinely interested in everybody's story. She's the kind of person who will ask a cabdriver in New York City if he has any kids. "What are their names?" she'll say. When I'm down, she shares my pain; for every new level of success I achieve, you can believe she's somewhere in the background, cheering louder and smiling broader than anyone else. Sometimes I feel like Gayle is the better part of myself—the part that says, "No matter what, I'm here for you." What I know for sure is that Gayle is a friend I can count on.

"If you don't know what your passion is, realize that one reason for your existence on earth is to find it."

SEPTEMBER
2001

"Everyone has the power for greatness—not for fame but greatness, because greatness is determined by service." Even before I first heard my all-time favorite quote from Dr. Martin Luther King Jr., I knew in my heart that the message was true. As far back as I can recall, my prayer has been the same: "Use me, God. Show me how to take who I am, who I want to be, and what I can do, and use it for a purpose greater than myself."

All of us need a vision for our lives, and even as we work to achieve the vision, we must surrender it to the power that is greater than we know. It's one of the defining principles of my life that I love to share: God can dream a bigger dream for you than you could ever dream for yourself. Before I understood that, I used to dream of having a salary to match my age—at 22, when I was earning $22,000 a year, I remember thinking that if I could just keep it up, I'd be making $40,000 by age 40. But the universe had a bigger dream for me, as it does for everyone reading these words. Success comes when you surrender to that dream—and let it lead you to the next best place.

What I know for sure is that if you want to have success, you can't make success your goal. As my friend Wintley Phipps, the gospel singer and minister, once told me, the key is not to worry about being successful but to instead work toward being significant—and the success will naturally follow. How can you serve your way to greatness? When you shift your focus from success to service, your work as a teacher, clerk, doctor, or dot-commer will instantly have more meaning.

We live in a world that confuses financial prosperity with success, dollars with the real deal of having a joy-filled life. By the late eighties, I had achieved fame, notoriety, Emmys, money, and houses with lots of things to put in them. I was prosperous, and yet a burning question nagged at me: What does all this mean? I've learned that possessions only have the meaning you give them. All my life, I'd been passing others' big homes and yachts while wondering, *What kind of person do you have to be to have all of that?* Now I know that if you'll just be yourself and follow your calling, success will lay itself before you in ways you never imagined. That doesn't mean we're all going to be yachting around the world. Real success means creating a life of meaning through service that fulfills your reason for being here.

Starting today, you can decide to have a life of significance by how you give of yourself to others. In his book *The Soul's Code,* James Hillman says that the way to true success is to honor your calling. Have the courage to follow your passion—and if you don't know what it is, realize that one reason for your existence on earth is to find it. It won't come to you through some special announcement or through a burning bush. Your life's work is to find your life's work—and then to exercise the discipline, tenacity, and hard work it takes to pursue it.

How do you know whether you're on the right path, with the right person, or in the right job? The same way you know when you're not: You feel it. Each of us has a personal call to greatness—and because yours is as unique to you as your fingerprint, no one can tell you what it is.

Ignoring your passion is like dying a slow death. Your life is speaking to you every day, all the time—and your job is to listen up and find the clues. Passion whispers to you through your feelings, beckoning you toward your highest good. Pay attention to what makes you feel energized, connected, stimulated—what gives you your juice. Do what you love, give it back in the form of service, and you will do more than succeed. You will triumph.

"The truth is that which feels right and good and loving. Love doesn't hurt. It feels really good."

JANUARY
2002

"Ye shall know the truth, and the truth shall make you free" has always been one of my favorite Bible verses—one I memorized long before I understood what it meant. I've since learned that you can't know the truth until you're willing to know yourself—and vice versa. Knowing yourself is a lifelong process, with your biggest lessons often emerging from your biggest mistakes.

My biggest mistakes in life have all stemmed from giving my power to someone else—believing that the love others had to offer was more important than the love I had to give to myself. I remember being 29 and in a relationship based on lies and deceit, down on my knees crying after Mr. Man walked out on me. I had been stood up for hours and dared to ask why. I remember him standing in the doorway and hurling these words at me: "The problem with you, baby doll, is that you think you're special." He then turned on his heels and slammed the door in my face.

As I huddled on the floor, the powerful words I'd memorized in childhood seemed to penetrate my being. In that moment I realized I didn't know a thing about the truth, but I knew I had to make it my business to find out. Why was I allowing myself to be treated this way? I had grown up watching my cousin Alice be abused by her boyfriend, and I had vowed I would never take such treatment. But now I saw with great clarity that the only difference between Alice and me was that I hadn't been physically hit. Mr. Man was wrong: I did not think I was special—and *that* was my problem. My lack of self-respect, my belief that I needed a man to make my life all right—that was also my problem.

Even with these insights, it took me another year to end the relationship. I kept hoping and praying things would get better, that he would change. I thought I could help him see that though I wasn't special, I could at least be useful. I was always doing things to make *him* feel special. None of it worked, so I started praying for strength to end it. I'd pray and wait to feel better. And wait. And wait. All the while repeating my same old patterns.

Until one day I got it. I knew the truth was that while I was waiting on God, God was waiting on me. He was waiting on me to make a decision to either pursue the life that was meant for me or be stifled by the one I was living. I recognized the truth that I am all right just as I am. I am enough all by myself.

That revelation brought its own miracle. Around that time the call came for me to audition for a talk show in Chicago—and soon after came *The Color Purple.* Possibilities kept unfolding before my eyes. If I'd stayed entangled in that relationship, my life as I know it would never have happened.

What is the truth of your life? It's your duty to know.

The truth is that which feels right and good and loving. Love doesn't hurt. It feels really good. It's that which allows you to live every day with integrity. Everything you do and say shows the world who you really are. Let it be the truth.

"A line Emily Dickinson wrote—'I dwell in Possibility'—has always meant so much to me."

FEBRUARY 2002

Whenever I hear Paul Simon's song "Born at the Right Time," I think he must be singing about me. I came into the world in 1954 in Mississippi—a state with more lynchings than any other in the Union—at a time when being a black man walking down the street minding your business made you subject to any white person's accusation or whimsy. A time when having a good job meant working for a "nice" white family that at least didn't call you nigger to your face. A time when Jim Crow reigned, segregation prevailed, and black teachers, themselves scarcely educated, were forced to use ragged textbooks discarded from white schools.

Yet the same year I was born, a season of change began. In 1954, the Supreme Court ruled in *Brown v. Board of Education* that blacks had the right to equal education. The ruling created hope that life could be better for black folks everywhere. That's why a line Emily Dickinson wrote, "I dwell in Possibility," has always meant so much to me.

I have always believed free will is a birthright, part of the universe's design for us. God even allows us to choose whether to be led by divine order. Slavery, the Taliban, and any other system that seeks to keep people from determining their own destinies are abominations.

Every soul yearns to be free. In 1997, while I was preparing to play Sethe in the movie *Beloved,* I arranged a trip along a portion of the Underground Railroad. I wanted to connect with what it felt like to be a slave wandering through the woods, making the way north to a life beyond slavery— a life where being free, at its most basic level, meant not having a master telling you what to do every minute. But when I was blindfolded, taken into the woods, and left alone to contemplate which direction led to the next "safe house," I understood for the first time that freedom isn't about not having a master. Freedom is about having a choice. In the film, Sethe explains what it was like to make the trek to freedom: "Looked like I loved [my children] more after we got here," she says. "Or maybe I knew as long as we were in Kentucky...they really weren't mine to love.... Sometimes I hear my boys, hear 'em laughing a laugh I ain't never heard. First I get scared, scared somebody might hear 'em and get mad. Then I remember that if they laugh that hard till it hurt, that be the only hurt they have all day." She also says, "I'd wake up in the mornin' and decide for myself what to do with the day," as if thinking: *Imagine, me decide.*

During shooting, I said those lines over and over, feeling the force they carried. In the years since, Sethe's words have remained with me—I rejoice in them daily. Sometimes they're my very first thought before I get out of bed. I can wake up in the morning and decide for myself what to do with the day—imagine, me decide. What a gift that is to all of us who live in the land of the free!

What I know for sure is that we all need to cherish that gift—to revel in it rather than take it for granted. After the hundreds of stories I've heard of atrocities around the globe, I know that if you're a woman born in the United States, you're one of the luckiest women in the world. Take your good fortune and lift your life to its highest calling. Understand that the right to choose your own path is a sacred privilege. Use it. Dwell in possibility.

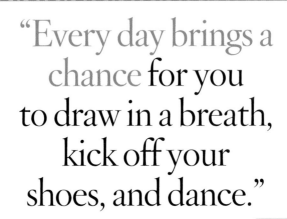

"Every day brings a chance for you to draw in a breath, kick off your shoes, and dance."

MAY
2002

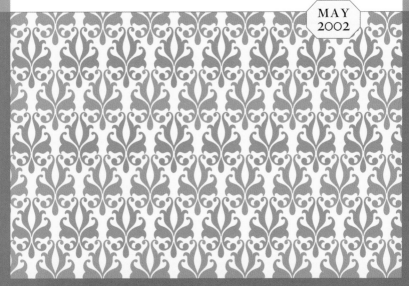

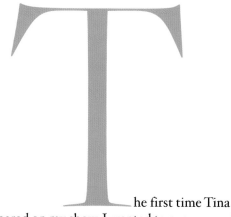he first time Tina Turner appeared on my show, I wanted to run away with her, be a backup girl, and dance all night onstage. Well, that dream came true one night in L.A. when the show went on tour with Tina. After a full day's rehearsal for just one song, I got my chance. It was the most nerve-racking, knee-shaking, exhilarating experience ever for me. For five minutes and 27 seconds I got a chance to feel what it's like to rock onstage. I have never been more out of my element, out of my body. I remember counting the steps in my head, trying to keep the rhythm, waiting for the big kick, and being so self-conscious. Then, in an instant, it dawned on me: *Okay, girl, this is going to be over soon.* And if I didn't loosen up, I would miss the fun of it. So I threw my head back, forgot about *step, step, turn, kick,* and

just danced. WHEEEEW! was that *fun*.

Several months later, I received a package from my friend and mentor Maya Angelou—she'd said she was sending me a gift she'd want any daughter of hers to have. When I ripped it open, I found a CD with a song by Lee Ann Womack that I can still hardly listen to without boohooing. The song, which is a testament to Maya's life, has this line as its refrain: *When you get the choice to sit it out or dance, I hope you dance.*

What I know for sure is that every day brings a chance for you to draw in a breath, kick off your shoes, and step out and dance—to live free of regret and filled with as much joy, fun, and laughter as you can stand. You can either waltz boldly onto the floor of life and live the way you know your spirit is nudging you to, or you can sit quietly by the wall, receding in the shadows of fear and self-doubt. You have the choice this very moment—the only moment you have for certain. Are you dancing in the light or languishing in the dark? If your life ended tomorrow, what would you regret not doing? If this were the last day of your life, would you spend it the way you're spending today? When was the last time you laughed with your girlfriend till your sides hurt or dropped the kids off with a sitter and went away for an entire weekend?

I once passed a billboard that caught my attention. It read HE WHO DIES WITH THE MOST TOYS IS STILL DEAD. Anyone who has ever come close to death can tell you that at the end of your life, you probably won't be reminiscing about how many all-nighters you pulled at the office or how much your mutual fund is worth. The thoughts that linger are the "if only" questions, like *Who could I have become if I had finally done the things I always wanted to do?*

The gift of deciding to face your mortality without turning away or flinching is the gift of recognizing that because you will die, you must live now. Whether you flounder or flourish is always in your hands—you are the single biggest influence in your life. And your journey begins with a choice to get up, step out, and live fully.

I hope you don't get so wrapped up in nonessential stuff this summer that you forget to really enjoy yourself—because this moment is about to be over. I hope you'll look back and remember this season as the time when you decided to make every one of your moments count, to relish each day as if there would never be another. And when you get the choice to sit it out or dance, I hope you dance.

"This is the body you've been given—love what you've got."

I still have the check I wrote to my first diet doctor—Baltimore, 1977. I was 23 years old, 148 pounds, a size 8, and I thought I was fat. The doctor put me on a 1,200-calorie regimen, and in less than two weeks I had lost ten pounds (there's nothing like the first time…). Two months later, I'd regained 12. Thus began the cycle of discontent, the struggle with my body. With myself.

I joined the dieting brigade—signing on for the Beverly Hills, Atkins, Scarsdale, Cabbage Soup, and even the Banana, Hot Dog, and Egg diets. What I didn't know is that with each diet, I was starving my muscles, slowing down my metabolism, and setting myself up to gain even more weight in the end. Around 1995, after years of yo-yoing, I finally realized that being grateful to my body, whatever shape it was in, was key to giving more love to myself.

Although I'd made the connection intellectually, living it was a different story. Then around last Christmas, after six months of unexplained heart palpitations, I finally got it. On December 19, 2001, I wrote in my journal: "One thing is for sure—having palpitations at night makes me more aware of being happy to awaken in the morning, more grateful for each day." I stopped taking my heart for granted and began thanking it for every beat it had ever given me. I marveled at the wonder of it: In 47 years, I'd never consciously given a thought to what my heart does, feeding oxygen to my lungs, liver, pancreas, even my brain, one beat at a time.

For so many years, I had let my heart down by not giving it the support it needed. Overeating. Overstressing. Overdoing. No wonder when I lay down at night it couldn't stop racing. I believe everything that happens in our lives has meaning, that each experience brings a message, if we're willing to hear it. So what was my speeding heart trying to tell me? I still didn't know the answer. Yet simply asking the question caused me to look at my body and how I had failed to honor it. How every diet I had ever been on was to fit into something— or just to fit in. Taking care of my heart, the life force of my body, had never been my priority.

I sat up in bed one crisp, sunny morning and made a vow to love my heart. To treat it with respect. To feed and nurture it. To work it out and then let it rest. Since

December I've kept that vow, and my body has started to redefine itself. One night when I was getting out of the tub, I glanced in the full-length mirror. For the first time, I didn't begin my critical speech. I actually felt a warming sense of gratitude for what I saw. My hair braided, not a stitch of makeup on, face clean. My eyes bright, alive. My shoulders and neck strong and firm. Every part of me thankful to be here, living through this body.

I did a head-to-toe assessment, and though there was plenty of room for improvement, I no longer hated any part of myself, including the cellulite. I thought, *This is the body you've been given—love what you've got.* This is the face I was born with—the same lines I had under my eyes at age 2 have gotten deeper, but they're my lines. The same broad nose I tried to heighten when I was 8, by sleeping with a clothespin and two cotton balls on the sides, is the nose I've grown into. The full lips I used to pull in when smiling are now the lips I use to speak to millions of people every day—my lips need to be full. In that moment, as I stood before the mirror, I had my own "spiritual transformation / a root revival of love," which Carolyn M. Rodgers writes of in one of my favorite poems, "Some Me of Beauty."

What I know for sure is that the struggle is over. I've finally made peace with my body.

"I've learned not to worry about what might come next."

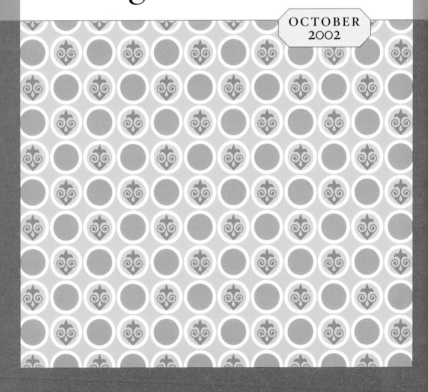

I'm not nearly as stressed as people might imagine. Over the years, I've learned to focus my energy on the present, to be fully aware of what's happening in every moment and not to worry about what should have happened, what's going wrong, or what might come next. Yet because I take in so much information and absorb so many people's stories every day, if I didn't find a way to decompress, I'd be totally ineffective—and probably a little crazy, too.

What I know for sure is that your breath is your anchor, the gift we've all been given to center ourselves in this very moment. Whenever I have an encounter that involves even the slightest tension, I stop, draw in a deep breath, and release. Ever notice how often you unconsciously hold your breath? Once you start paying attention, it might surprise you to see how much tension you've been carrying around inside. Nothing is more effective than a deep, slow inhale and release for surrendering what you can't control, and focusing again on what's right in front of you.

None of us is built to run nonstop. That's why, when you don't give yourself the time and care you need, your body rebels in the form of sickness and exhaustion. How do I give back to myself? Hardly a day goes by that I don't talk things out with my best friend, Gayle, right down to the last little details. Almost every night, I soak in a hot bath and enjoy at least one lit candle. It may sound hokey, but focusing on a burning candle for a minute while taking deep and relaxing breaths is very calming. In the evenings right before sleep, I don't read or watch anything—including late-night news—that would add anxiety. And because I don't like fitful dreams, I protect my sleep by dealing with difficult situations during my waking hours. I also keep a gratitude journal and, at the end of a workday, I "come down" by reading a great novel or just sitting with myself to come back to my center—it's what I call going mindless.

Taking care of yourself so you can better care for others is an idea many women I talk to still can't embrace. Two years ago when life coach Cheryl Richardson was on my show introducing the concept of self-care—putting your own needs ahead of anyone else's—the audience literally booed! Women were upset with her for even suggesting that their needs come before their children's.

I interrupted to explain: Cheryl didn't say to abandon your children and let them starve. She was simply suggesting you nurture yourself so you'll have more nurturing to give to those who most need you. It's the oxygen-mask theory: If you don't put on your mask first, you won't be able to save anyone else. Stop. Go mindless. Breathe. Let go. And remind yourself that this very moment is the only one you know you have for sure.

"The same questions follow every woman through girlhood and adolescence: Can I really do this? Will I get it right? Am I okay?"

NOVEMBER 2002

I first learned about sex the year I was 9. I was living in Milwaukee that summer, staying at an uncle's home, when a 19-year-old cousin raped me. As I trembled and cried, he took me for ice cream and convinced me not to tell—and for 12 years I didn't.

It was a very long time before I understood how completely my life had been changed—how in one instant, I was no longer a child. When you are sexually violated, it's not the physical act that destroys you. It's the weight of the secret you feel you have to keep, the person you have to become so no one will discover what you're hiding. It's losing a sense of appropriate boundaries and unconsciously confusing mistreatment with love. It's holding on to the belief I had all the way into my 30s that

I had done something to cause the abuse. That I was a bad girl. The single greatest feeling I carried with me through childhood was of being alone.

I spent most of my teenage years trying to convince myself of my worth by becoming the smart girl, the nice girl, the one who spoke well before an audience and earned excellent grades. Both then and in my 20s, I sought validation from men who meant me no good. I gave my power away to those whose offer of love was more important than the love I had to give to myself.

A teenager's sense of herself comes from how respected and valued she felt as a girl—and that begins the moment she enters the world. Before a child can even talk, she looks to her parents and other adults to confirm that she counts, that her existence means something. Toni Morrison once told me that when a child's parents enter a room, that child is unconsciously asking herself, *Do my mom's and dad's eyes light up when they see me? Do they think I matter?* I believe that when a teenage girl seeks gratification in the arms and eyes of sexual partners, she is ultimately seeking what we all crave—connection. And as I've talked with scores of parents and experts over the years and reflected on my own experience, I've learned that a teenage girl is often seeking that connection through promiscuity because something in her home life is awry.

Part of the wonder and beauty of childhood is that every experience is new. I remember the first time I was allowed to wash the dishes—my grandmother put a little stool in front of the sink so I could reach. I recall being so afraid I'd drop a dish that it would accidentally slip from my hand and smash to the floor. I wondered, *Can I really do this? Will I get it right? Will I be okay?*

Adolescence is all about discovering your individuality—stumbling along as you learn who you are in the world, and deciding how your values differ from your parents'. What I know for sure is that the same questions I asked myself as I stood at the sink follow every woman through girlhood and adolescence. When a teenage girl seems unreachable and is making choices that threaten her, that's exactly when she most needs her parents to move closer to her, not back away. At her core, she is still just a girl who's asking, *Can I really do this? Will I get it right? Am I okay?* I know for sure that the most valuable gift a loved one can offer is a resounding yes.

"The world can only value mothering to the extent that women everywhere stand and declare that it must be so."

MAY 2003

I'm in awe of good mothers — those heroines all around me who sacrifice daily out of love for their children. In our society, we give motherhood plenty of lip service. We pat moms on the head, bring them flowers on Mother's Day, and honor them before crowds. But at the end of the day, we don't extend them the same respect we would a professor, a dentist, an accountant, or a judge. Women who choose full-time mothering are often put in a box by their friends and former colleagues — a container labeled JUST A MOM.

I believe the choice to become a mother is the choice to become one of the greatest spiritual teachers there is. To create an environment that's stimulating and nurturing, to pass on a sense of responsibility to another human being, to raise a child who understands that he or she is created from good and is capable of anything—I know for sure that few callings are more honorable. To play down mothering as small is to crack the very foundation on which greatness stands.

The world can only value mothering to the extent that women everywhere stand and declare that it must be so. In our hands, we hold the power to transform the perception of motherhood. Whether we decide to work full-time while raising children, stay home with our kids, or bear no children at all, we need to understand that any put-down of the decision to mother is a threat to women's choices everywhere. We should no longer allow a mother to be defined as "just a mom." It is on her back that great nations are built. We should no longer allow any woman's voice to be drowned out or disregarded. As we affirm other women, and as we teach our sons, husbands, and friends to hold them in the highest regard, we honor both the mothers whose shoulders we've stood on and the daughters who will one day stand tall on ours.

In May—and every other month of the year—I honor and thank every great spiritual teacher who goes by the name of Mother.

"For me, doubt means don't. Don't move. Don't answer. Don't rush forward."

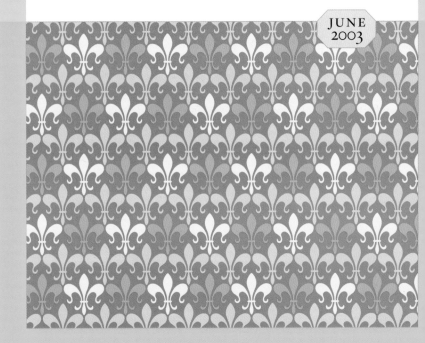

I n my early years of
television, I was often overwhelmed by people's view
of me as a benevolent caregiver. Some would spend their
last dime on a bus ticket to get to me, children would
run away from home, abused women would leave their
husbands and just show up at the doorstep of my studio,
all hoping I'd help. In those days, I'd spend a lot of energy
trying to get a girl back to her family or hanging on the
phone with someone who was threatening to kill herself.
Every week I was bombarded by organizations that
wanted me to rescue them financially. I found myself
writing check after check, and over time that wore on my
spirit. I was so busy trying to give all that everyone else
needed me to offer that I lost touch with what I had a
genuine desire to give. I finally had to stop and consider

what I believe is one of the most important questions a woman can ask herself: *What do I really want—and what is my spirit telling me is the best way to proceed?*

My answer eventually led me toward my passion for serving women and girls. I have a deep understanding of what it's like to be a girl who has suffered abuse or lived in poverty, and I believe that education is the door to freedom, the rainbow that leads to the pot of gold. I began to realize that in order to be most effective, I had to be extremely focused on using my time, my concern, my resources, and my compassion to uplift a generation of courageous women who own themselves and know their strength. I knew I couldn't save every dying child or intervene in every case of abuse. None of us can. But once I got clear about what I most wanted to give, much of what didn't line up with that intention naturally fell away.

Those years of becoming focused taught me a powerful lesson about tuning in to my gut— that inkling that says, *Hold on. Something's not right here. Please pause and make an adjustment.* For me, doubt often means don't. Don't move. Don't answer. Don't rush forward. When I'm mired in confusion about what the next step should be, when I'm asked to do something for which I feel little enthusiasm, that's my sign to just stop—to get still until my instincts give me the go-ahead. I believe that uncertainty is really my spirit's way of whispering, *I'm in flux. I can't decide for you. Something is off-balance here.* I take that as a cue to re-center myself before making a decision—a reminder from above to wait for confirmation. When the universe compels me toward the best path to take, it never leaves me with "Maybe," "Should I?" or even "Perhaps." I always know for sure when it's telling me to proceed— because everything inside me rises up to reverberate "Yes!"

"For the first time in my adult life, I feel part of a community."

NOVEMBER
2003

I've never been a social person. I know this may come as a surprise to most people, but ask anyone who knows me well—Stedman, Gayle—and they will confirm it's true.

I've lived in Chicago for 19 years, and I can count on one hand, and still have some fingers remaining, the number of times I've visited friends or met for dinner, or gone out just for fun. I've always kept downtime for myself and a wee circle of friends I consider my extended family.

I've lived in apartments since I left my dad's house. Apartments where I often didn't take the time to know the person across the hallway, let alone everyone on my floor. We were all too busy.

Recently, I moved to a new neighborhood. Not an

apartment but a house. A whole world has opened to me. I've become social. For the first time in my adult life, I feel a part of a community. As I was pushing my cart down the cereal aisle at Vons, a woman I didn't know stopped me and said, "Welcome to the neighborhood. We all love it here and hope you will, too." She said it with such sincerity that I wanted to weep. Nobody had ever said those words to me before.

In that moment, I made a conscious decision not to move into my house and close the gate as I have for so many years living in the city, shutting myself off to even the possibility of a new circle of friends. I now live in a neighborhood where everybody knows me and I know them.

First Joe and Judy, who live next door, invited me over for Joe's homemade pizza and said it would be ready in an hour. I hesitated only for a moment. I put on my flip-flops, headed over makeup-less and in my sweats, and ended up staying the afternoon. This was whole new territory for me. Bordering on adventurous. Chattin' it up at a stranger's house, not for TV but just to find our own common ground.

Since then, I've had tea with the Abercrombies, who live three doors down. Been to a backyard barbecue at Bob and Marlene's…a pool party at Barry and Jelinda's…watermelon martinis at Julie's…a rose garden gathering at Sally's. A formal sit-down at Annette and Harold's with more silverware than I could manage. A rib-cooking contest at Margo's, which I deserved to win but didn't. Watched the sunset and ate black-eyed peas at the Nicholsons'...and attended an all-out feast under the stars with 50 neighbors at the Reitmans'. I knew all but two of them by first name. I've become verrrrrry social.

My life has a new, unexpected layer. I thought I was through making friends. Much to my surprise, though, I've found myself looking forward to hanging out, laughing, talking serious, but often just connecting and embracing one another as a part of the circle. It's added new meaning, a feeling of community I didn't even know I was missing.

What I know for sure is that everything happens for a reason—and the stranger who approached me in the grocery store with such feeling triggered something: the possibility that I could make this new neighborhood a real home and not just a place to live.

I've always known that life is better when you share it. I now realize it gets even sweeter when you expand the circle.

"All these years I've been feeling like I was growing into myself. Finally, I feel grown."

ow, I can hardly
believe it's here! I made it. Fifty. Me. My first and
foremost reaction is *hallelujah!!!* I'm so grateful. I think of
all the notable and noteworthy people who didn't see 50.
Those we knew as icons, like the John Kennedys, father
and son. Princess Di. Dr. King. And the many and mighty
whose names will never make the history books but are
beloved by those who knew them. I think of the 9/11 angels
who were our earth peers for too short a time. And my
heart overflows with gratitude for my great big life at 50.

What I know for sure as I crest this major milestone:
My life is bigger than I can ever know or imagine. It has
its own force field. I can feel myself propelling it—
guiding it, even. But most often I try to surrender to its
own divine guidance.

What I've learned in this first 50 is that if you can allow yourself to breathe into the depth, wonder, beauty, craziness, and strife—everything that represents the fullness of your life—you can live fearlessly. Because you come to realize that if you just keep breathing, you cannot be conquered. Divorce, trauma, disease, disappointment...I remember a time when I was so devastated by a friend's betrayal that I didn't even want to get out of bed. But I breathed my way through it and came out on the other side, stronger.

You can take from every experience what it has to offer you. And you cannot be defeated if you just keep taking one breath followed by another. I've seen this many times in my own life and a thousand times over in the lives of others. Maybe you watched a show I did in November with a young woman named Jacqui, who was burned alive when the car she was riding in was hit by a drunk driver. She's had more than 40 operations and basically has no face— it melted away in the raging flames. A paramedic at the scene who heard her screams said he prayed for God to take her so her suffering could be over.

Burned on more than 60 percent of her body, Jacqui survived. And how! One breath at a time, she kept healing herself, through the most excruciating pain and scarring. She told me she only allows herself five minutes a day to cry. She said she has to keep getting up and moving forward. When I asked her if there were times she wished she'd died in that fire, she said, "No, I have too much left to do." I got goose bumps sitting before this woman with the face of a tortured soul and the heart of an angel. I knew in that moment that I was looking at the living, breathing definition of inner beauty, inner strength, and love of self. And if she feels she has a lot more to do, then I, with every advantage in life—the primary ones being my health and the ability to take care of myself—had better get busy.

All these years I've been taking lessons from life experiences and feeling like I was growing into myself. Finally, I feel grown. More like myself than I've ever been. If it's true what Maya Angelou says, that the 50s represent everything you were meant to be, all I can say is, watch out.

I've been meaning to be more focused. To pay attention to everything. To take absolutely nothing for granted. Dance more often. Celebrate something every day. Give back to the world what it has given to me. My heart is open to the future. Bring it on!

"If you feel incomplete, you alone must fill yourself with love in all your empty, shattered spaces."

I've been racking my brain for weeks over what I know for sure about love. Let's face it: Love's an intimidating subject that's been done and overdone, trivialized and dramatized to the point of mass delusion about what it is and isn't.

This is what I know for sure: The screenwriters of that movie *Love Actually* had the right idea, their premise being that love is all around. The chance to love and be loved exists no matter where you are. Most of us can't see it because we have our own preconceived ideas about what it is (it's supposed to knock you off your feet and make you swoon) and how it should appear (in a tall, slim, witty, charming package). So if love doesn't show up wrapped in our personal fantasy, we fail to recognize it.

I know this for sure: Love is.

It exists in all forms.

Sometimes I walk into my front yard and I can feel all my trees just vibrating love. I know love is always available for the asking. I've seen so many women (and been one myself) dazed by the idea of romance, believing they're not complete unless they find someone to make their lives whole. When you think about it, isn't that a crazy notion? You, alone, make a whole person. And if you feel incomplete, you alone must fill yourself with love in all your empty, shattered spaces.

Ralph Waldo Emerson said, "Nothing can bring you peace but yourself."

I've often witnessed people pining away to be in love with somebody, to be rescued from their daily lives and swept into romantic bliss, when all around there are children, neighbors, friends, and strangers also yearning for someone to know they matter. Look around and notice—possibility is everywhere.

I was rushing from the CNN building recently into the cold night after doing *Larry King Live.* I wasn't wearing a coat, so I was focused on one thing—getting to my car. A guy across the street yelled my name; I didn't notice at first, so he shouted louder: "Oprah, Oprah, can you see me? I'm here. Show me some love."

Now, this was a total stranger I'll probably never see again, but he caused me to pause and think. I'll bet a lot of people feel the way he did as they watch others around them absorbed in whatever seems to matter in the moment.

If you find it a strain to open your heart full-throttle

to the Big L, start in first gear: Use compassion for a while and feel yourself shifting to something deeper. Before you know it, you'll be able to be a blessing of understanding, empathy, caring, and love.

When you make loving others the story of your life, there's never a final chapter, because the legacy continues. You lend your light to one person, and he or she shines it on another and another and another.

"Getting my lifelong weight struggle under control has come from a process of treating myself as well as I treat others in every way."

AUGUST 2004

I s there anything I love more than a good meal? Not much. I was in Rome recently, eating as the Romans do, at a delightful little community restaurant—all Italians except for our table: Reggie, Andre, Gayle, her daughter, Kirby, and me. There was a moment when the waiters, prompted by our Italian host, Angelo, brought out so many delicious antipasti that I actually felt my heart surge, like an engine switching gears. We had zucchini stuffed with prosciutto, and fresh, ripe tomatoes layered with melting mozzarella so warm you could see tiny cheese bubbles, along with a bottle of Sassicaia '85, a Tuscan red wine that had been breathing for half an hour, to sip and savor like liquid velvet. Oh my, these were moments to treasure!

Did I mention I topped all this off with a bowl of pasta

e fagioli (this bean, tomato, and pasta dish is my all-time favorite when done well, and this was perfection) and a little tiramisu? Yep, that was some good eatin'. And I paid for it, too, with a 90-minute jog around the Colosseum the next day—but it was worth every delectable bite.

I have a lot of beliefs. The value of eating well is one of them. I know for sure that a meal that brings you real pleasure will do you more good in the long and short term than a lot of "filler" food that leaves you standing in your kitchen, roaming from cabinet to fridge. I call it that grazing feeling: You want something but can't figure out what it is. All the carrots, celery, and skinless chicken in the world can't give you the satisfaction of one good piece of chocolate if that's what you really crave.

So I now eat one piece—maximum, two—and dare myself to stop and relish it, knowing full well that "tomorrow is another day, Scarlett," and there's more where that came from. I don't have to consume the whole box just because it's there. What a concept!

Getting my lifelong weight struggle under control has come from a process of treating myself as well as I treat others in every way. I've learned that you can't eat junk and expect to have an unjunked life. It's true that you are what you eat, what you think, what you believe, what you do. Eating well, making healthy choices, delicious choices, enticing choices is symbolic of how you treat yourself, and it shows. Your skin, your hair, your eyes, your energy level, your attitude, are all affected by what you ingest.

After my Roman splurge, I came home, worked out

consistently, and ate a lot of salads — fresh greens, picked from my own garden, thank you very much. I used the simplest dressing ever: two tablespoons of extra-virgin olive oil, one crushed garlic clove, and the juice from half a lemon. I ate grilled artichokes, also homegrown, and soups made from whatever was available in the garden — tomato, basil, and red pepper; summer squash; green pea. And for one meal a day, I had a protein dish of grilled fish or chicken. It wasn't pasta e fagioli, but it was still delicious and satisfying.

Even today, as I finished my spinach salad — wilted with hot olive oil and balsamic vinegar, and layered with thin slices of shaved Parmesan — and put down my fork, there was just a trace memory of that melted mozzarella in Rome. Now, that was a meal worth the wait and the workout. I'm looking forward to returning and doing as the Romans do.

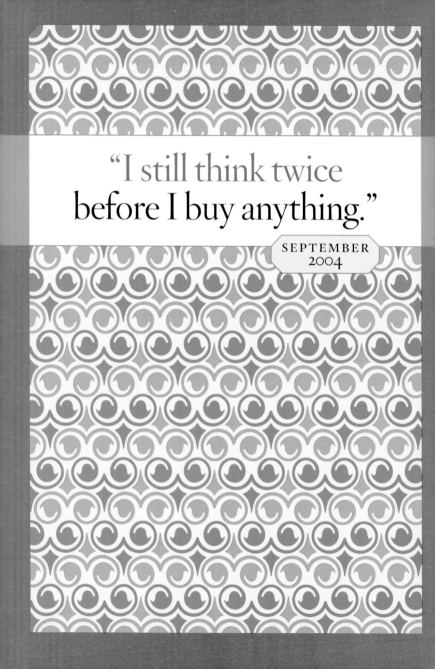

"I still think twice before I buy anything."

SEPTEMBER
2004

I've lived in every salary range, starting at $100 a week and moving up to $10,000 a year, then 12, 22, 50, 100, 225, and beyond.

My father raised me to believe that debt was a terrible thing. In our house, it was akin to a character flaw, like laziness and what he called trifling. So when I moved away from home and was $1,800 in debt within a year, I felt I'd failed. I never told my father, nor would I have dared to borrow money from him. So I took out a consolidation loan at 21 percent interest, ate a lot of raisin bran for dinner, and bought the cheapest car I could afford—a bucket on wheels, I used to call it, but it got me to and from work. I tithed 10 percent to the church and shopped for clothes only once a year.

I paid off the $1,800 and vowed never again to create

more bills than I could pay. I just hated the way overspending made me feel—anxious, like I couldn't fulfill my obligations. Irresponsible.

My dad saved for everything that mattered—a washer and dryer, a new refrigerator. When I left home in Nashville in 1976, he still hadn't gotten a new TV. He said his "money wasn't right." When my show went national, that's the first thing I bought him—a color TV, paid for in cash.

I still think twice before I buy anything. How will this fit in with what I already have? Am I just caught up in the moment? Can it be of real use to me or is it just something beautiful to have (which, if one can afford it, is a very legitimate reason)? I *loooove* beautiful things. Last month I was in an antiques store and the dealer was showing me a gorgeous 18th-century dressing table with mirrors and hidden drawers. It was polished to such a sheen that the cherrywood seemed to be vibrating. But as I stood pondering whether to purchase it, I said to the guy, "You're right, it's beautiful and I've never seen one quite like it, but I don't really need a dressing table with all that razzle-dazzle." He took a pretentious breath and replied, "Madam, no one buys anything here because of their needs—these are treasures to be enjoyed." Indeed. *Well, let me get down to the "needs" store,* I thought, *because what I'm really looking for are fireplace utensils.* Not only did I not need a dressing table, I hadn't the space for it. But Mr. Dealer had a point. Some things are just to be treasured and enjoyed.

And I know for sure that you enjoy everything a lot

more when you're not overreaching. This is how you know you've shopped smart: You bring home a purchase and there's not a tinge of remorse, and whatever you got feels better to you ten days later than it did when you first bought it.

I feel blessed to be in the unbelievable position of being able to buy anything, *anything* I want. I remember the first time this occurred to me. In 1988 I was in Tiffany's trying to decide between one china pattern and another. I was going back and forth, and finally my shopping buddy said, "Why don't you just get both? You can afford to." *Oh my God...I can. I can. I can get both!* I started jumping up and down in the store like I'd won the lottery.

Since that time, I've had many one-or-the-other dilemmas. Often I force myself to choose (upbringing) or decide which friend I can give the other to. More than anything, I hate waste. Uselessness. The things you buy represent how you see yourself—how you wish for people to see you.

You're a smart cookie. Let the world know it.

"Listen.
Pay attention.
Treasure
every moment."

The whole idea of connection fascinates me. No doubt we're all more digitally and fiber-optically linked than ever before, but we're apparently losing our real connections.

I've seen it coming for a while—haven't you? You can't get through dinner or walk down the street without someone pulling out a cell phone. I often wonder, *Who in the world is everybody talking to?*

Just recently, going through the turnstile in Borders, I watched a mother talking and laughing with her cell phone in one hand—and with the other, dragging her crying 3-year-old, whose coat had gotten stuck in the door. She was too busy chatting it up to notice. Major disconnect.

As hard as I've tried not to fall prey to cellular mania (I still don't carry a phone around), I have succumbed to the life-changing advantages of the BlackBerry. I'm not a "crackberrian" yet, but I could use some withdrawal therapy. I first noticed this when someone snapped a picture and showed it to me in living color: My friends Gayle and Andre and I were sitting in a store in Rome waiting for Gayle's daughter, Kirby, to try on a pair of jeans. We weren't talking to one another—we were all on our BlackBerries. *Oh, no, I've become one of those people,* I thought. Those people who are in a conversation with you but, as you're obviously not holding their interest, take the call from the phone that's ringing Beethoven's Fifth at 78 rpm and continue to talk to whoever's on the other end. Those people who are sitting in a restaurant and checking voice mail every 15 minutes. Those people who are not in the moment but always looking to see, What's next? What else should I be doing?

Notice the next time you're giving your friend, mate, child, or coworker less than your full self. I'll bet it happens more often than you're aware. With to-do lists a mile long and constant deadlines, it's no surprise that most of us feel cut off not only from our partners and loved ones but also from ourselves. Our lives are busier, faster—and we're moving further away from our center.

I know for sure that the way to feel connected in all relationships is to stay attuned to the Source, which I believe is the energy that vibrates through all life. You can never stray too far from what is really meaningful before losing connection with yourself and everybody else. And when you've lost that, neither AT&T nor the best Verizon hookup can bring it back.

Meditate. Breathe consciously. Listen. Pay attention. Treasure every moment.

Make the connection.

☐ 44 and hot?

☐ 44 and not?

Can women be hotter
at 40 than 20?